Analytics:
Sports Stats
& More

HOOP-FALL

Jason Smith

Trajectory Accuracy   45%

Shot Accuracy   (54/72) 75%

2 Pointers   (6/10) 60%

3 Pointers   (20/32) 62%

Free Throws   (3/9) 33%

ARC TRAINER

Data set

12.11.13 - Game
12.11.13 - Training

SHOT
FREQUENCY

ArcAid.

Cambridge Consultants

SHOT FREQUENCY AND SU

CAREERS
OFF THE FIELD

MC

Analytics: Sports Stats and More

By Matt Marini

Mason Crest

450 Parkway Drive, Suite D
Broomall, PA 19008
www.masoncrest.com

Series ISBN: 978-1-4222-3264-4
Hardback ISBN: 978-1-4222-3265-1
EBook ISBN: 978-1-4222-8523-7

3 5 7 9 8 6 4 2

Produced by Shoreline Publishing Group LLC
Santa Barbara, California
Editorial Director: James Buckley Jr.
Designer: Bill Madrid
Production: Sandy Gordon
www.shorelinepublishing.com

Cover photo: ArcAid by Cambridge Consultants

Library of Congress Cataloging-in-Publication Data
Marini, Matthew, 1970-
        Analytics : sports stats and more / by Matt Marini.
        pages cm. -- (Careers in Sports)
        Includes webography.
        Includes index.
    ISBN 978-1-4222-3265-1 (Hardback) -- ISBN 978-1-4222-3264-4 (Series) -- ISBN 978-1-
4222-8523-7 (Ebook) 1. Sports--Vocational guidance--Juvenile literature. 2. Statisticians--
Vocational guidance--Juvenile literature. 3. Sports--Statistics.
    I. Title.
    GV734.3.M36 2015
    796.023--dc23
                                        2015009961

CONTENTS

Key Icons to Look For

 Words to Understand: These words with their easy-to-understand definitions will increase the reader's understanding of the text, while building vocabulary skills.

 Sidebars: This boxed material within the main text allows readers to build knowledge, gain insights, explore possibilities, and broaden their perspectives by weaving together additional information to provide realistic and holistic perspectives.

 Research Projects: Readers are pointed toward areas of further inquiry connected to each chapter. Suggestions are provided for projects that encourage deeper research and analysis.

 Text-Dependent Questions: These questions send the reader back to the text for more careful attention to the evidence presented here.

 Series Glossary of Key Terms: This back-of-the-book glossary contains terminology used throughout this series. Words found here increase the reader's ability to read and comprehend higher-level books and articles in this field.

Foreword
By Al Ferrer

So you want to work in sports? Good luck! You've taken a great first step by picking up this volume of CAREERS OFF THE FIELD. I've been around sports professionally—on and off the field, in the front office, and in the classroom—for more than 35 years. My students have gone on to work in all the major sports leagues and for university athletic programs. They've become agents, writers, coaches, and broadcasters. They were just where you are now, and the lessons they learned can help you succeed.

One of the most important things to remember when looking for a job in sports is that being a sports fan is not enough. If you get an interview with a team, and your first sentence is "I'm your biggest fan," that's a kiss of death. They don't want fans, they want pros. Show your experience, show what you know, show how you can contribute.

Another big no-no is to say, "I'll do anything." That makes you a non-professional or a wanna-be. You have to do the research and find out what area is best for your personality and your skills. This book series will be a vital tool for you to do that research, to find out what areas in sports are out there, what kind of people work in them, and where you would best fit in.

That leads to my third point: Know yourself. Look carefully at your interests and skills. You need to understand what you're good at and how you like to work. If you get energy from being around people, then you don't want to be in a room with a computer because you'll go nuts. You want to be in the action, around people, so you might look at sales or marketing or media relations or being an agent. If you're more comfortable being by yourself, then you look at analysis, research, perhaps the numbers side of scouting or recruiting. You have to know yourself.

You also have to manage your expectations. There is a lot of money in sports, but unless you are a star athlete, you probably won't be making much in your early years.

I'm not trying to be negative, but I want to be realistic. I've loved every minute of my life in sports. If you have a passion for sports and you can bring professionalism and quality work—and you understand your expectations—you can have a great career. Just like the athletes we admire, though, you have to prepare, you have to work hard, and you have to never, ever quit.

Series consultant Al Ferrer founded the sports management program at the University of California, Santa Barbara, after an award-winning career as a Division I baseball coach. Along with his work as a professor, Ferrer is an advisor to pro and college teams, athletes, and sports businesses.

Introduction

Words to Understand

articulate: express using clear and exact phrasing

ERA: earned run average—a baseball statistic measuring the number of earned runs a pitcher allows per nine innings

general manager: in sports, the person in charge of putting together the roster of the team

relief pitcher: a pitcher who comes into a game after a starting pitcher is removed

Ari Kaplan has made his life in sports, but he has never been paid for playing the game. In the late 1980s, Kaplan was a college student at the California Institute of Technology (Caltech). He was on the baseball team, but knew he did not have a major-league future . . . or so he thought. At Caltech, he studied math and computer science. That knowledge, combined with a lifelong love of baseball, put him on a different path. It all started when he thought about something concerning the statistics of baseball that had bothered him for a few years.

"As a [New York] Mets' fan, I remember some of the pitchers, from watching the games, seemed to have good **ERA**s," Kaplan recalls. "I wondered how, if a **relief pitcher** came into the game with the bases loaded and allowed three runs to score, it could show '0' runs allowed at the end of the box score? Why does he have a zero if he let in three runs?

"It was just common sense to me, from watching the game, that did not seem accurate. I came up with a way to more effectively describe what a pitcher does. That was basically what it was. I saw a relief pitcher blow a game, saw that his ERA was 0.00 for that game, and I said, 'That doesn't make sense.' Everything else sprouted from that."

Kaplan wrote a letter to the Los Angeles Dodgers' general manager, Fred Claire, who was impressed with Kaplan's concept.

"Ari came in and said, 'I don't think the ERA for relief pitchers makes any sense,'" recalls Claire. "He said he wanted to develop a formula, a statistical formula, to give a better understanding of this situation. He asked to speak with the pitchers and coaching staff. That is how he came up with the research. Our pitchers, especially the starters, were very interested in what would happen when those three hitters were on base."

Kaplan called his new rating Reliever Effectiveness (RE). The stat evaluated for the first time how well relievers come into a game and got batters out. It was one of the first big breakthroughs in a movement to go beyond the traditional stats that you see on a baseball card. Reliever Effectiveness looked at a question: When a reliever comes in with runners on base, how effective is he at getting the runners out?

"If you are a starting pitcher," Kaplan says, "and you leave the game with the bases loaded, those three base runners will be charged to you if they score. It's completely dependent upon the relief pitcher. So a starting pitcher's ERA can vary ten, twenty, or even thirty percent based off what the relief staff does.

Before analytics, managers went with their gut when making decisions about pitching changes. Today, they have a mountain of numbers at their fingertips to help them make the right call.

"So if you are a **general manager** [GM] and you want to look at a pitcher, you want to know how that pitcher would perform on your staff, with your relievers, and with your defense behind you. A thirty percent swing of ERA is huge, and having more accurate information will help you make a better decision. It is what I called the 'Expected ERA' because it gives the GM a better understanding—and it also gives the fans a better understanding—of what is actually happening."

Creative use of statistical analysis helped Ari Kaplan have his Dodgers' dreams come true.

Kaplan took his research and interviews with the Dodgers and made a career. "I was able to **articulate** it so effectively that Caltech allowed me to present to the [school's] Board of Trustees," says Kaplan. "I explained what I thought was a better system of evaluating pitchers. It was a big thing to say that a billion-dollar industry was not using the best analytics.

"So I gave the presentation, and a guy raises his hand and says, 'Hi, I'm the owner of the Baltimore Orioles, and I'd like to hire you.' My response was, 'I don't know who you are. Thank you so much, and to the people in the back of the room, don't let that man walk out the door until I talk to him!'

"We met after the talk, and he said he was serious. Then we had a formal interview, and he hired me."

Kaplan showed that with a little initiative, he was able to turn an interest into his life's work. His story of how he made sports analytics—the use of advanced stats and data to create new ways of looking at sports performance—has been repeated over and over in the years since by experts in a wide range of fields. Sports is not just for heavy-lifting, hard-throwing, superstar athletes. The business of sports needs new ideas—ideas that are being created in the field of sports analytics.

Words to Understand

concessions: the shopping opportunities—food, drink, merchandise, and services—available at a sporting event

Getting Started

As sports evolve in the twenty-first century, wins and losses are no longer decided just by the athletic ability of the players. So what is the edge that teams seek? In a new, computer-driven age, it's the numbers. The science of sports analytics is revolutionizing the games people watch and play.

Of course, coaching matters, and having players with great natural ability further enhances the team's ability to win. So many players, however, are gifted, and so many teams have good coaches. At the highest levels, teams are so evenly matched that even a tiny advantage can make a huge difference.

In Major League Baseball, for example, it is pretty much accepted that every team will win at least 62 games and every team will lose 62 games. (It is rare for a team to win more than 100 games or lose more than 100 games in the 162-game season.) What happens in those other 38 games is what puts a team in

Winning means more fans in the seats, so teams are looking at analytics for new paths to victory.

the playoffs, or has it at the bottom of the standings. Can new types of information help make more of those 38 games into wins?

When a team wins, it makes the fans happy. In addition, it also builds a larger fan base, which then leads to more customers in the seats, more cars in the parking lots, more people buying **concessions**, etc. Winning leads to more money, which leads to profits. Owners are wealthy people, and they like to make even more money, while watching their team win as well, of course.

There is a lot involved in running a team. It takes more than players and some gear. It takes business savvy, good marketing, and top people in the front office. Having better players on the field is the obvious way to increase your victory total. The more good/great players you have, the more likely you will win. However, everyone knows that, and if everyone is looking for the best players, you need to do more.

What about more coaching? Teams have looked for wins by adding more coaches. In 2014, the Seattle Seahawks had 23 assistant coaches. It was not long ago that most teams did not have more than a dozen. Today, most NFL teams have about 20 assistant coaches.

If everyone has great players, and the teams have the coaches to help develop them, where else can they look for an edge? The place to improve has become the front office. In the last 10 to 15 years, many teams have begun to uncover information that may not be obvious to the other teams in their league.

In basketball, is there a difference when a team has a certain five-man lineup on the court compared to other combinations? In baseball, shifting defenses has become commonplace as teams force the opposing hitters to power the ball into the heart of the shift or have them adjust and alter their swing. In soccer, new information about how much players run and move on the field during a game has altered training techniques.

Off the field, teams are doing research to help players perform at ultimate efficiency. For example, some teams have developed sleep patterns for their players, which becomes important when teams travel and land in a new city in the middle of the night. Other teams value nutrition for their players. Sure, clubhouses may still have snacks for the players, but more and more often the snacks are no longer candy bars but have been replaced by fruit, vegetables, energy shakes, and other healthy options. The reason for all these changes is the new approach that teams are taking, by using science to help their players. One of those sciences is math, and math is the key to sports analytics.

The field of sports analytics is growing by leaps and bounds. Some people estimate that within the next decade, every pro sports team, and even many top college programs in the major sports, will have 10 or more people working on analytics in the front office. The jobs are coming; here are some steps to get ready for them.

Education

With the growth of sports analytics has come numerous college courses designed to train people for that work. Here is an example of one such sports analytics class from Columbia

University: "This course is an examination of the most advanced applications of [data]. The structure of the course is to examine the use of them to four

main areas of interest: player performance measurement, in-game decision making, player selection/team building, and general administration such as marketing, pricing, contracts, stadium management, etc. Emphasis will be placed on not only how the application of analytics has improved each of these situations, but how those decisions relate to business decisions in any other field of commerce."

Already these courses are turning out people who have made analytics into a career. The top two people in the analytics department of the NFL's Jacksonville Jaguars are Tony

Students with talent in advanced math can combine that with a love of sports to find careers in analytics.

Bill James

In the mid-1970s, Bill James was a security guard working the night shift at a pork-and-beans cannery in Kansas. James was a big baseball fan, and absolutely loved statistics. In the age before computers and the Internet, James began to gather as many baseball statistics that he could find.

After the 1976 season, James wrote and published the *1977 Baseball Abstract: Featuring 18 Categories of Statistical Information That You Just Can't Find Anywhere Else*. His book was 68 photocopied pages stapled together and cost $3.50. He put an ad in *The Sporting News* and was thrilled when he sold 75 copies.

The following year, James sold 250 copies. By 1982, his annual book was in bookstores nationwide. James then became the creative director of STATS LLC, one of the first national organizations to gather and analyze sports information. Eventually, fans, media companies, and baseball experts were buying James' book and following his research. Today, James is regarded as the godfather of sports analytics.

Kahn, who studied finance in college, and Daniel Adler, who majored in economics and served as president of Harvard's sports analysis collective. Ari Kaplan, who studied math at Caltech, owns his own analytics company, Ariball, and has co-authored five best-selling books on analytics, databases, and baseball. In addition, he teaches an online baseball analytics course.

Kaplan suggests that "classes on statistical analysis, big data, and databases would help prepare for a career." Math departments have many ways to learn how to handle large amounts of data. Computer programming might also be helpful since computers are the tools to manipulate and study the information. Business classes help students understand the role of different departments in an organization. How does the marketing department use data as opposed to how the shipping department uses it? Sports management classes teach students the structure of pro or college sports organizations. It's important to know how each type of business runs. Simply being a great math student is not enough; a sports analytics professional has to be able to use and share discoveries in the context of what his or her organization needs.

Internship, Anyone?

As with most types of business, you need more than a classroom or book education. Nothing helps prepare a person more than real-life, day-to-day work. Internships are the lifeblood of many businesses, and the front offices of sports teams are no exception. An intern is usually not paid in money, but in experience. The internship gives a person the chance to learn, but can very often lead to full-time employment. There is nothing better for an employer than to hire someone they already know can do the job. On the other hand, if the intern realizes during the internship that the job wasn't quite what was expected, he or she can walk away with no regrets.

Internships can be difficult to obtain because there are numerous other people in the world who are interested in the same field as you. In the summer of 2013, the Jacksonville Jaguars received more than 100 applications for their training-camp internships. If you are willing to become an intern and work in a front office for a summer, be persistent. Do not give up after the first or second "no."

First Steps

Begin by having an idea of what you are trying to accomplish. If you are in high school or college and are looking for six to eight weeks of a summer internship, start searching as soon as possible. Even if summer is eight or nine months away, that is a good time to begin reaching out to teams.

Call the team and find out who makes the hiring decisions. Ask for the spelling of their names and titles. Double-check this information on the Internet. If your information does not match, call the team back and again request the information. There is nothing worse than spelling someone's name incorrectly, especially in your first letter or email. Also, using the correct title is a sign of respect. If you are a hard worker and make sure you have the facts correct, you are more likely to get hired.

Your introductory letter should be short and to the point. Focus on your academic skill set and not on your love of the team or of sports. Teams are looking for serious professionals, not fans. If you want to make analytics or stats the focus of your internship, show that you understand what that work is by mentioning relevant classwork or work with your school sports teams.

Sports analytics professionals will be judged on their work and skill with numbers, but business skills such as interviewing, running meetings, and writing well also are valuable.

Moneyball

While Fred Claire was using analytics in the late 1980s, and a few other front offices around baseball were utilizing information, it was not until 2003, when the book *Moneyball* was released, that the industry went from grassroots to front page.

If you have not yet read *Moneyball*, and have any interest in this industry, it is a must read. The book discusses the concepts and ideas of Oakland Athletics general manager Billy Beane. In the early 2000s, despite having one of baseball's smallest payrolls, the A's continued making it to the postseason year after year. Writer Michael Lewis weaves a wonderful story, providing a perspective unknown to most of us prior to the book's release.

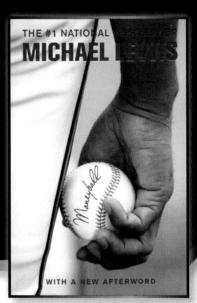

This eye-opening tale, while not universally embraced by every baseball executive, more or less did open the eyes of most baseball front offices. In addition, it forced other sports to begin examining the way they approach their specific sport. It led to an explosion of analytics in all professional sports leagues.

In addition to your letter, you need to send along your résumé, no matter how little experience you may have in the work world. Show your résumé to a counselor. It is always suggested to have one or more people review your résumé. Do not let it exceed one page, and be honest. Any exaggerations or mistakes on a résumé usually lead to immediate removal from the job opportunity.

Use networking to find out more. Rory Davidson was in high school in Menlo Park, California, and used a family connection to get some meetings with the people at the San Francisco 49ers who were introducing various levels of analytics to the team. "I spent a day with them talking about how the NFL values draft picks based on which round a player is chosen," says Davidson, who now studies at the University of Oregon. "We've stayed in touch, and I've been able to see the people I met there at the sports analytics conferences I've been to."

Text-Dependent Questions

1. When should you begin looking for internships?
2. According to Ari Kaplan, what are some of the types of classes and software you should be familiar with?
3. What was Bill James' job when he began writing and self-publishing his annual baseball book?

Research Project

Start looking at teams near you for internship opportunities. Don't forget minor-league teams in sports such as baseball, basketball, or hockey. The opportunities might not be in analytics, but learning other parts of a sports organization can be helpful.

Words to Understand

arbitration: the process of having an approved outsider decide a disputed point in business or law without using the court system

methodology: the process through which a particular task or series of tasks is accomplished

metric: a measurement involving numbers

Rule V Draft: in baseball, the selection of players who are not on a team's 40-man roster but have been in pro ball for at least four or five years

vulnerable: able to be hurt or injured

Hard at Work

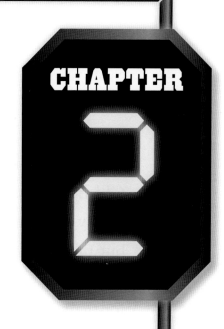

CHAPTER 2

Sports analytics professional Ari Kaplan of Ariball.com recalls what happened to him after the Baltimore Orioles hired him in college. "When I was a teenager, [Orioles manager and Hall of Fame player] Frank Robinson was one of my first bosses. Another was Roland Hemond, a general manager also honored by the Hall of Fame. It was great to work with such outstanding baseball people. One of the big honors I had was meeting Earl Weaver [pictured at left], the legendary manager who was one of the innovators in splits, which is the practice of looking at lefty-righty matchups [in determining batting order and which players would face which pitchers]. Weaver had these index cards he would bring into the dugout, so he was one of the first to do it. One of my first big honors was to computerize that entire methodology for the Orioles. I would then print it out for the coaches every day."

From those early days of transferring information from note cards to computer programs, analytics has exploded in size and complexity. For example, STATS LLC, which is one of football's leading analytic companies, tracks more than 90 separate bits of data in a single play. As Tony Khan of the Jacksonville Jaguars told *ESPN The Magazine* in a phrase that could be echoed in nearly every sport, "There's a ton of information in football, but that's the problem." With all that information, teams need people to sort through the data and determine what is relevant for their specific organization.

Analytics: Here to Stay

Former Dodgers manager Fred Claire, who now works as a partner with Ari Kaplan at Ariball.com, knows analytics is here to stay. "Part of the reason averages and offense are down in baseball is because pitching analytics has utilized more weaknesses in the hitters than vice versa," says Claire. "Pitchers see where hitters are **vulnerable** via analytics. But if a hitter has a great report on [Dodgers' Cy Young Award winner] Clayton Kershaw, good luck!"

Kaplan notes that from a baseball perspective, your job duties could vary vastly. "On the baseball side, I've had every

The Jacksonville Jaguars (left) are one of the NFL teams that has embraced the potential of sports analytics.

role you can think of in the front office," says Kaplan. "From player and roster evaluations, to payroll information, from major-league practices to opening training academies in the Dominican Republic.

"One of the most fun things is helping the team and the coaching staff prepare for a game—sitting down and coming up with a game plan. Let's say, with the opposing pitcher: How are we expected to do? How is he against the lineup the first, second, third, fourth time? When should each of the relievers and the closer come in? That is part of game planning."

The NBA now has SportVU, a creation of STATS LLC that is being used in every NBA arena. The data it captures can help answer almost any type of question regarding the players:

NBA teams use stats to analyze opponents so that stars such as John Wall (2) can find new ways to attack the basket.

Who cannot fight through a pick on defense? What players don't move without the ball on offense? Who doesn't block out on a rebound? Anyone working in basketball analytics needs to know how to interpret that data.

Back in the late 1980s, Claire was at the forefront of wanting more information than most teams. "I believe in analytics," he says, "and there is a fellow by the name of Craig Wright, who reached out to me when I became the general manager. Even before Craig, I was attracted to Bill James. I was a person who wanted to acquire all the information that I could.

"Craig Wright had worked with the Texas Rangers. I always believe in having the best scouts. When I became the general manager, I made some changes; it was Craig who had the information on minor-league players. I hired Craig because I wanted that viewpoint. At the time, it would have been outlandish. Of course, I never played professionally, and Craig never did, but that didn't frighten me, because I just wanted his information."

With the help of executives such as Claire and Billy Beane of the Oakland A's, baseball led

Elias Sports Bureau

Created in 1913 and based out of New York City, the Elias Sports Bureau is the Official Statistician for the National Football League, Major League Baseball, the National Basketball Association, the National Hockey League, Major League Soccer, and the Women's National Basketball Association.

The Elias Sports Bureau is also the primary source of statistics for ESPN, Turner Sports, the NFL Network, and other networks and media outlets. It provides information to many major Web sites, too. Much of the information and graphics you see during a game—for example, comparing the statistics of a specific player with those of someone 15 years ago—was developed by the historical and number-driven minds of the Elias Sports Bureau.

the way in incorporating stats and analytics in a more organized way. That practice has expanded throughout pro sports.

Not Just Baseball

Baseball indeed led the way, but every sport has caught the analytics bug. In golf, analytics has helped the media and general public clearly understand some aspects of the game. For example, "strokes-gained putting," a performance **metric** that Mark Broadie helped develop with the assistance of students at the Massachusetts Institute of Technology (MIT), has been embraced by the PGA Tour and is used during broadcasts. It calculates the number of putts a golfer takes relative to the tour average, taking into account the initial putting distance. At the end of the round, the tournament, and the season, it spits out a stat that shows the fine line between failure and success.

In the NBA, there are still questions within the sport as to how much analytics can determine a player's value. A 2005 quote by writer Chris Ballard explains that "every action on a basketball court is influenced by nine other players, not to mention a coach. For this reason, there is no 'Holy Grail' in basketball equivalent of baseball's on-base percentage." That is changing rapidly, as a host of complicated formulas is put into play. Being able to track dozens of stats from each player each game through the use of computer programming has changed how teams approach the draft, game strategy, and more. Just the graphics alone created by the data-gathering have helped fans see which players shoot better from certain spots or how a particular defense can help cut down an opponent's shooting percentage.

Pro golfers use information gathered from putting stats and more to adjust their games and win.

In hockey, the sport is attempting to determine the best way to grade goaltenders. Per NHL.com, Columbus Blue Jackets goaltending coach Ian Clark says the position may be too much for a single statistical measure because there are so many outside variables that can affect each goalie's statistical performance.

"Goalies react to the hand dealt to them," Clark told NHL.com. "They don't get to control play. Unlike a quarterback or a pitcher, who gets to control and dictate the play, goaltenders are recipients of the play, and as such there is a huge impact on how the team plays in front of them and statistical outcomes. Goalies face completely different things and have no control over it, whereas Peyton Manning controls what is going on over his playing surface when he lines up behind the ball. That affects statistics, and that is one of the reasons goaltending is a bit of an anomaly when it comes to using pure numbers."

Pro football is perhaps lagging a bit behind the other leagues in intensive use of analytics. The 2015 "Analytics" issue of *ESPN The Magazine* included no NFL teams on its list of franchises that were "all-in" on analytics. By comparison, nine Major League Baseball teams earned that ranking. However, that tide might be shifting as more coaches who grew up with thinking in terms of analytics take on more responsibilities.

Hockey analysts have found that using analytics on goalies poses some interesting challenges.

A Hand in Everything

As Kaplan summarizes, one reason why he loves his job so much is because of its ever-changing landscape. "A typical day in this life is that there is not a typical day in this life," Kaplan says. "You help prepare for games, and above and beyond that, play a big role in helping the general manager, depending on the time of the season. If it is the **arbitration** season, you are preparing for cases, if winter meetings are coming up, you are preparing for the **Rule V Draft** and the amateur draft, so there is a kind of a rhythm to the season. So the typical day in the life changes depending on what month it is, and what decisions are coming up—if it is free-agency time, or if it is time for September call ups, what players make the most sense, things like that.

"That is what is so fun. There are so many things to do, and it varies a lot. Even when it's time to hire a new manager, I have helped prepare interview questions for managerial candidates."

On a different scale, University of Oregon student Rory Davidson learned that being around the teams adds to the skill set of analytics people. He provided stats and information to his high school's football coaches, but he got a lot of information in return.

"I didn't learn the analytics from working with the football team, I learned those skills in classrooms," Davidson says. "But from the football team itself, I learned how to 'talk football.' Not all coaches are open to all these numbers. Instead of throwing numbers at them, you have to be able to talk like them and put the information into words and terms they use. I came into it knowing a lot of football, but working with the team took it to that next level."

As Davidson and other young people work toward joining the Ari Kaplans of the world, learning how to combine the words of sports with the numbers of sports will prove to be a vital tool.

Text-Dependent Questions

1. What was Ari Kaplan's first big move in putting stats into computers for the Orioles?

2. Why did Ian Clark say it is a challenge to compare hockey goaltenders?

3. What are some of the aspects of an NBA game that analytics can now explore thanks to SportVU?

Research Project

If you were helping your favorite team interview managerial/coaching candidates, what types of questions, from an analytics standpoint, would you want them to answer?

Words to Understand

Excel: a computer program that creates spreadsheets and is able to handle many different kinds of data

homestand: a series of smaller series in which a sports team plays several teams in a row without leaving its home ballpark

Realities of the Workplace

CHAPTER 3

The goal of working in sports starts early and often can be inspired by a desire to keep playing. However, after the reality hits that 99.9 percent of the world does not have the ability to play at the pro level, there are still ways to be part of the team. Being part of a team is not always glamorous, however. Pro sports is a business, and even if analytics is your part in it, expect to work long and hard.

Consider that if you are traveling with the team, you might be leaving the ballpark at night at the conclusion of a **homestand**. Around midnight, after packing up at the ballpark, you would take a bus to the airport, fly to the next city, take another bus to the hotel, check in at four or five o'clock in the morning, and then be up and running later that day for a game at night. Three or four days later, you do that all over again. That's just baseball.

In the NBA, teams sometimes play four games in five nights in four different cities.

The NFL regular season usually lasts from September to December. The analytics season never stops. Analytics has now reached the point where teams are using it to help with the interview process at the NFL Scouting Combine each February in Indianapolis. The stats people then prepare for the April NFL Draft. Summer brings decision time for veterans, and some of that information comes from the programmers. As the regular season looms, the workload only increases, peaking during the grind of a 17-week season.

It's time-consuming work, but it pays off. Kaplan cites the impact a traveling analytics person can have on a team. "The analytics and advance scout are blending together," he says, "so many teams have a guy that helps provide information, whether that is advanced video or analytics.

"For instance, in my case, I provide a baseball manager with crucial pieces of information. For example, this opposing pitcher has not thrown consecutive pickoff attempts to a base in the last two years. That is huge information that you would want to know. So if the manager buys in, he could demand that someone travels with the team to bounce things off of. I think every team would want that, and the teams that don't are at a disadvantage."

Pro team sports are not the only places that demand a lot of time from stats

Football in shorts? Working in the NFL is not just for the fall; it's a year-round occupation.

The Seattle Sounders (right) brought in an expert from Microsoft to help them get a handle on analytics.

analysts. Golf has perhaps too much data. ShotLink has been in full use by the PGA since 2003, and has recorded more than 10 million shots, dissecting information into various categories. Amazingly, ShotLink features 58 stats for tee shots alone. Someone has to gather that data, analyze it, and prepare reports. Experts travel with the tour, which goes to a different place each weekend for nearly 10 months. In fact, pro golf is played somewhere around the world year-round. There are no off-season breaks for golf stat analysts.

Major League Soccer (MLS) has also joined the analytics world. Seattle Sounders head fitness coach Dave Tenney explained his situation to Grantland.com. "As time has gone on, I think we've done a pretty good job of it, but the sports science pretty much consisted of me, my laptop, an **Excel** spreadsheet, and an external hard drive. Now, we have match analysis data and more in-match data as well. It reached a point where we are getting more data, and we have more questions. We have outgrown the system we had in place because of the amount of data that we are collecting on a daily and weekly basis."

Tenney hired Ravi Ramineni, a former Microsoft engineer, to help sort through all the data on another level. "Where I step in is to help the coaching staff mix and sort this data so they can use it in their decision making," Ramineni says. "The data has been collected, but coaches need it in a way where they can visualize it better or have the statistical analysis done."

Fred Claire says that from a general manager's perspective, there is a balance between all of the information and knowing how to use it. "The use of information is to make the best decision," he says. "The only real question in all of that is to define and utilize what is there." That is why teams may be hiring more people to help determine how to make the best use of all of the information being developed today.

A Season Out of the Sun

Each sport has its own schedules and pace, but here's a look at the schedule from a baseball perspective. The dates might vary from sport to sport, but the workload will not.

If you are working with a Major League Baseball team, the games are about three hours long, but don't think your day is only from the first pitch to the final out. You have more than seven weeks of spring training, which entails 30 or so games, including split-squad games at different locations in either Florida or Arizona. On the surface, that sounds great, especially if you live in a cold-weather climate. However, realize that you will be away from your home for that period of February and March. Do you have a family you will be leaving behind? If you live alone, do you have a pet that needs to be fed and walked?

"The schedule of a baseball front office analyst varies with the time of year," says Ari Kaplan of Ariball. "The pattern of spring training, the regular season, the amateur draft, hopefully the postseason,

One plus of working in baseball analytics: You'll probably enjoy a little time in the sun at spring training in Florida or Arizona.

free agency, organizational meetings, the winter meetings, and arbitration hearings set the workload. During the regular season, you are typically working during the games and one to two hours after the end of the game. The GM and field staff return from the game and often have postgame decisions they might need your advice

A baseball office: The Cleveland Indians sports analytics staff poses at the ballpark near a mural of old-time action.

on. Often you are there from nine in the morning until one o'clock at night, then you do it all again the next day."

Life in the Office

The vast majority of a sports analytics professional's time will be in an office environment. In the last 20 to 30 years, most sports franchises have moved into new arenas. These clubs most likely have nicer amenities than clubs that have been in the same venue for decades. So while you most likely won't have a choice as to where your "office" is located on site, just realize you might be sitting in a dark room with no windows in the depths of a stadium for multiple hours per day. There could be four or five interns in the same room for long hours, too.

You will be spending a lot of time sitting in a chair staring at a computer screen. That is not necessarily the healthiest combination. With your 16-hour days, believe it or not, trying to watch what you eat and drink will be a daily challenge if you want to stay healthy. Tony Khan of the Jacksonville Jaguars even had a daybed installed at the stadium so he could at least sleep on a mattress instead of the floor or couch. How much time might you spend at work? Khan lists the football stadium as the home address on his driver's license.

Upside of working for an NFL team such as the Jaguars? Good seats for the game. Downside? Like Tony Khan, you might hardly ever leave the stadium offices.

"One of the challenges for people looking to get into the front offices of sports teams is the sacrifice of a balanced lifestyle and family," Kaplan says. "Baseball requires long hours, unexpected calls, and meetings day and night and weekends. If you're married, having a supportive and understanding family will be beneficial as you embark on your journey for the days, months, and years ahead."

People interested in an analytical job will take into account all those factors as they consider whether to make it a part of their career.

Other Angles

Claiming a place in the hard-working, numbers-crunching world doesn't have to go through sports. Many people have come into sports analytics after solid careers in other fields. Young people have entered the arena not after making all-star teams, but after earning academic honors far from the playing field.

Sig Mejdal studied computer science and pyschology, then worked at Lockheed Martin and NASA. He still loved baseball, however, and in 2005, moved into the front office of the St. Louis Cardinals. Today, he is director of decision science for the Houston Astros.

The Jaguars' Tony Khan started his career in finance and later worked with a biodiesel company. Even the University of Kentucky men's basketball team brought a full-time analytics pro on board, hiring Joel Justus in 2014 from his previous job as a high school coach.

Around the sports world, people are looking outside the usual channels for the ideas that will change their games. That's even the message that young future analysts are hearing.

Rory Davidson, the University of Oregon student aiming for such a career, says, "It's interesting that for many of the people that I've talked to in this area, the recurring theme was that you don't have to start in sports. Many people are hired from other analytics jobs in completely different fields—medical or business or social media. So if your first job out of college isn't with the Forty-Niners, it's not the end of the world or the end of your hope for getting into sports, too."

Persistence, hard work, sticking with your dream: It sounds as if making it in sports analytics calls for the same sort of personal traits needed to make it in sports itself.

Text-Dependent Questions

1. Name three sections of the typical baseball season that would involve the use of analysis.

2. Describe a possible typical day for a baseball stat analyst, in terms of time.

3. How many different statistics does ShotLink generate just from PGA tee shots?

Research Project

Just as a warm up to doing analytics yourself, try to build some new data sets. Pretend you have an internship with your high school football team. The coach wants an analysis of your team's offensive strategy from the previous season. Dig out the box scores of all the games and make charts or graphs that show:

• in which quarters the team scores the most points;

• the ratio of run plays to pass plays on offense;

• the average number of yards per play gained per game.

Words to Understand

imperative: very important

The Nitty-Gritty

The beauty of analytics, former Dodgers' GM Fred Claire says, is that "unlike scouting, analytics is not someone's opinion, it is fact based."

The need to be able to think outside the box is **imperative** if you want to be involved in analytics.

CHAPTER 4

Case Studies

To look at how analytics impacts sports, here are some examples of data in action.

During the 2011 NFL Draft, the Atlanta Falcons traded two first-round draft picks, one second-round pick, and two fourth-round choices to move up and select wide receiver Julio Jones (pictured at left) with the sixth overall pick. It was a move that was questioned by many, but the Falcons had used analytics to help determine the value of the draft picks they traded. The Falcons had found that less than 15 percent of fourth-round selections become NFL starters, so in their mind it was essentially a three-for-one trade. Jones since has become one of the NFL's top pass-catchers.

Another NFL example: Teams need to be able to determine what the coaching staff needs, then supply the data. Jacksonville's Tony Khan created a stat for defensive players called "Passes Touched per Target," which was determined by the number of

A statistical analysis of his game helped Brandt Snedeker become one of the top-ranked golfers in the world.

throws a player intercepted and deflected, divided by the number of pass attempts thrown in his direction. By using this formula and reviewing college players entering the draft, the Jaguars selected Connecticut cornerback Dwayne Gratz in the third round in 2013. Cornerback is a premium NFL position in which most starters are first-round picks, but Gratz was a starter in each of his first two NFL seasons. Using new stats to dig deeper is the reason most teams are embracing the practice.

Pro golfer Brandt Snedeker explained the power of analytics for him on the PGA Tour. He entered the 2012 British Open having missed the cut in all three of his previous Open starts. His stats, however, said it should be otherwise. Mark Horton, an English numbers wizard, crunched Snedeker's data and developed a plan.

"[Horton] said, 'Let me break it down for you,'" Snedeker told golf.com. "He told me that I don't drive it particularly straight, but I drive it okay. I don't hit a bunch of greens, but I hit them okay. 'But you putt really freakin' good—you're one of the best I've ever seen. So you know what you need to do this week? Just hit the danged green!'"

That sounds like simple advice, but for Snedeker, it was seeing it spelled out in numbers that made the difference. He was indeed over-swinging his tee shots and second shots. By cutting back on that, his game immediately improved. He tied the 36-hole British Open scoring record and went on to finish third. Later that season, he won the Tour Championship and the FedEx Cup. Once the thirty-fifth-ranked player in the world, Snedeker soared to number four, a surge that began with a discussion about statistics.

The future for sports analytics is incredibly bright. Snedeker is living proof. Thanks to the stats-driven improvement in his game, he earned nearly $12 million from 2012 through 2014. Talk about impact!

The Future

While some baseball teams more than others have embraced the industry for years, other sports are looking for that "competitive edge" that can help their franchise to gain that advantage.

The NFL remains the elephant in the room. Some football teams are beginning to have their practices analyzed, to see if they are spending their time working on the plays that most impact a game. For example, are teams spending only five percent of their practice time on special teams plays when those events actually make up 13 percent of the game action?

When it comes to football, many agree that we are in the infancy stages of analytics. "There were times when we all wondered if football would ever get it," John Pollard, the general manager of STATS LLC's Sports Solutions Group, told *ESPN The Magazine* a few years ago. "Once football grabs hold of analytics—and that's where we are heading—it can redefine the sport."

How much do special teams plays such as field goals affect games? NFL analytics are still trying to put a number on some of that information.

In baseball, some experts say defense is the new frontier for analytics. New methods of measuring success or failure are being created.

While baseball is awash in analytics, many aspects of the industry are still not fully explored. "Defensive metrics are largely untapped," says

Kaplan regarding baseball. "This [2015] season it is expected that Major League Baseball is going to provide an immense amount of defensive data, and teams will need to tackle that. What is the value of a plus-defensive shortstop? Is it a million dollars? Two million? How does it affect how you position players? How does that change your game strategy?"

College baseball is an unknown because some Division I schools have the technology at their ballparks, "but most smaller schools do not," says Kaplan. "They are getting some funding and looking to grow." That would allow teams to blend scouts and analytics when looking at college players for the upcoming draft.

Eventually, the more fields that have the data cameras in place will provide much more information that needs to be dissected and analyzed. If a lot of colleges end up with cameras to track information, it will further encourage big-league teams to evaluate amateur players with the technology used to dissect the professionals.

Dean Oliver, who used to work for the NBA's Denver Nuggets and is now ESPN's director of production analytics, points out that with SportVU, "the data will be there for every team to use however it wants—including making mistakes.

Here's a number old-timers and new-age thinkers can agree on: the speed of a pitch, which here hit 98 miles (157 km) per hour.

The uncertainty comes less from lack of data than from lack of analytic power. Decisions will continue to be made, some using 'guts,' some using data, and the best ones using the right blend of both."

Claire says that while analytics tells a story, scouts will always have a place in the game. "There are some scouts who are very good at analyzing pitchers, and others who are better at analyzing hitters, so as a GM I have to figure out how to scout the scout," he says. "If you are considering trading for a player, or drafting a player, you need to know what kind of character he has. How competitive is he? Does he play hurt? Does he stay out? You have to have both the analytics and the scouting perspective."

Do you believe your eyes or do you believe the data? At first controversial, sports analytics are now an established part of the industry. The data experts have already redefined sports. Finding out how analytics works and where your skills and interests fit in might redefine your future, too.

Text-Dependent Questions

1. What is the name of the stat Tony Khan created to rate college cornerbacks?
2. Per Ari Kaplan, why are college baseball analytics still relatively untapped?
3. What golfer used stats to take a big step forward in his career?

Research Project

Try to think of a statistic that you would like analyzed in any sport. Do some digging on the Internet to see what type of information you can find to help formulate your study. Try to invent a stat that no one has thought of!

Find Out More

Books

Keri, Jonah. *The Extra 2%: How Wall Street Strategies Took a Major League Baseball Team from Worst to First.* New York: Ballantine Books/ESPN Books, 2011.

Lewis, Michael. *Moneyball: The Art of Winning an Unfair Game.* New York.: W.W. Norton, 2002.

Web Sites

www.esb.com/
Elias Sports Bureau, one of the oldest sports stats companies.

Baseball Analytics
www.edx.org/course/sabermetrics-101-introduction-baseball-bux-sabr101x
Ari Kaplan's Baseball Analytics course; check with your school, as this might be used for college credit.

stats.hockeyanalysis.com/
Hockey Stats

www.advancedfootballanalytics.com/
Football Analytics

www.mlssoccer.com/news/analytics
Soccer Analytics

grantland.com/features/expected-value-possession-nba-analytics/
This is a great article that breaks down how the NBA uses analytics.

Series Glossary
of Key Terms

academic: relating to classes and studies

alumni: people who graduate from a particular college

boilerplate: a standard set of text and information that an organization puts at the end of every press release

compliance: the action of following rules

conferences: groups of schools that play each other frequently in sports

constituencies: a specific group of people related by their connection to an organization or demographic group

credential: a document that gives the holder permission to take part in an event in a way not open to the public

eligibility: a student's ability to compete in sports, based on grades or other school or NCAA requirements

entrepreneurs: people who start their own companies

freelance: a person who does not work full-time for a company, but is paid for each piece of work

gamer: in sports journalism, a write-up of a game

intercollegiate: something that takes places between two schools, such as a sporting event

internships: positions that rarely offer pay but provide on-the-job experience

objective: material written based solely on the facts of a situation

orthopedics: the branch of medicine that specializes in preventing and correcting problems with bones and muscles

recruiting: the process of finding the best athletes to play for a team

revenue: money earned from a business or event

spreadsheets: computer programs that calculate numbers and organize information in rows and columns

subjective: material written from a particular point of view, choosing facts to suit the opinion

Index

Credits

About the Author

Matt Marini has been around sports and stats for nearly two decades. He was an editor with NFL Publishing and has contributed to numerous national publications. He also is the project manager for the National Football League's *Record & Fact Book*, an annual publication that offers historical and new information on all 32 NFL teams and the Pro Football Hall of Fame, as well as an extensive records section.